The Beauty of Hopi Jewelry

By Theda Bassman

Photography by Gene Balzer

Pendant of Two Horn Priest Kachina edged with pink coral, lapis lazuli, coral and turquoise.

Bracelet with lapis lazuli, coral and sugilite.

Necklace with Tibetan turquoise stone.

All made in 1991 by Roy Talaheftewa.
Courtesy of Museum of Northern Arizona Gift Shop.

Front Cover Photo

Two-sided pendant with Kokopelli Kachinas on one side and maze design on the other side. Made in 1993 by Floyd Namingha. Courtesy of Turquoise Village.

Bracelet with Bisbee Turquoise stone made in 1993 by Harold Lomayaktewa. Courtesy of Turquoise Village.

Pin with spider and water symbols made in 1993 by Marsha Josytewa. Private collection.

Ring with Kokopelli Kachina made in1992 by Leroy Honyaktewa. Private collection.

Belt buckle with sun and eagle made in 1993 by Verden Mansfield. Courtesy of Roxanne and Greg Hofmann.

Earrings with prayer feather design made in 1988 by Raymond Kyasyousie.Private collection.

Kiva Publishing, Inc.
21731 East Buckskin Drive
Walnut, California

Copyright ©1993 by Theda Bassman

Printed in Hong Kong
9 8 7 6 5 4 3

ISBN 1-885772-01-7

Dedication ◆

This book is dedicated to my other children

Chena, Harold, Robin and Cecil.

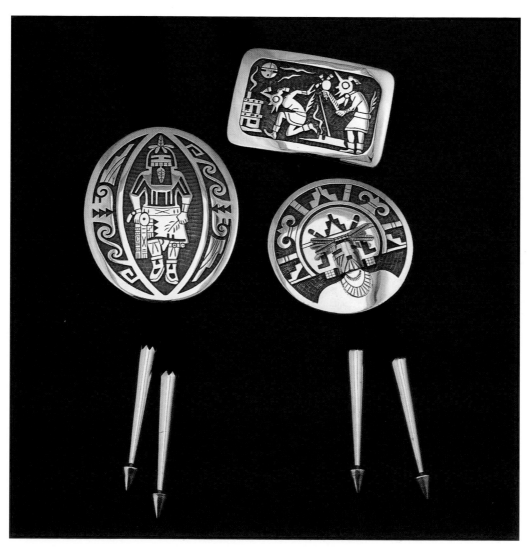

Belt buckle with Mud Head Clowns made by Verden Mansfield.
Oval bola tie with Long-haired Kachina made by Ben Mansfield.
Round bola tie of Shalako Kachina made by Lawrence Saufkie.
All made in 1992. Private collection.

❖ ——————————————— Acknowledgments

My thanks to the following people who so graciously permitted their jewelry to be photographed:

> Ula and Lee Beaudry
> Shirley and Marvin Bowman
> Dine and Bob Dellenback
> Gordon Graff
> Roxanne and Greg Hofmann
> Al Myman
> Gary Newman
> Louise Riley
> Mae Secakuku
> Beverly Sekaquaptewa
> Selmer Collection

And all of the private collectors who wish to remain anonymous.

Additional thanks to the galleries and museums and their staffs who provided me with jewelry and help:

> Calnimptewa Gallery, Oraibi, Arizona
> Heard Museum Shop, Phoenix, Arizona
> Hopi Gallery, Second Mesa, Arizona
> Monongya Gallery, Oraibi, Arizona, with special thanks to
>   Marlinda Velasco
> Museum of Northern Arizona Gift Shop, Flagstaff, Arizona
> Museum of Northern Arizona Collection, Flagstaff, Arizona
> Puchteca, Flagstaff, Arizona
> Southwest Gallery, Chicago, Illinois
> Tanner's Indian Arts, Gallup, New Mexico
> Turquoise Village, Zuni, New Mexico

Thanks to Margaret Nickleson Wright for writing her book, *Hopi Silver* and to Barton Wright for his book, *Hallmarks of the Southwest.* Both books were a tremendous help to me in the identification of the artists.

A special thanks to Greg Hofmann, at Turquoise Village, Zuni, New Mexico, who not only made his entire inventory available to me whenever I wished, but who also was instrumental in obtaining exceptional jewelry from collector friends and organizations for inclusion in the book.

My thanks to my wonderful photographer, Gene Balzer, who manages to capture with his camera all that I want to say.

Lastly, my heartfelt thanks to my husband, Michael, who is the soul of patience in helping me with proofreading, over and over again, and for his suggestions after reading all that I had written.

Introduction

The Hopi Indians have developed a unique style of jewelry making. The designs and concepts are part and parcel of the Hopi religion, life, and ceremonies. Many of the designs depict water in its various forms. Since the land of the Hopi is arid, there is a focus on water needed for their crops and for drinking.

Their jewelry is called overlay and is quite distinctive. It is made by cutting a design out of one piece of silver and soldering it onto a plain sheet of silver. The design is then oxidized with liver of sulfate to produce beautiful shadows and shading.

Originally Hopi jewelry resembled the jewelry of the Navajo Indians. However, in 1947 Paul Saufkie and Fred Kabotie were successful in getting the Federal Government to fund programs to train Hopi G.I.s of World War II in the making of overlay jewelry. This led to the opening of the Hopi Silversmith Cooperative

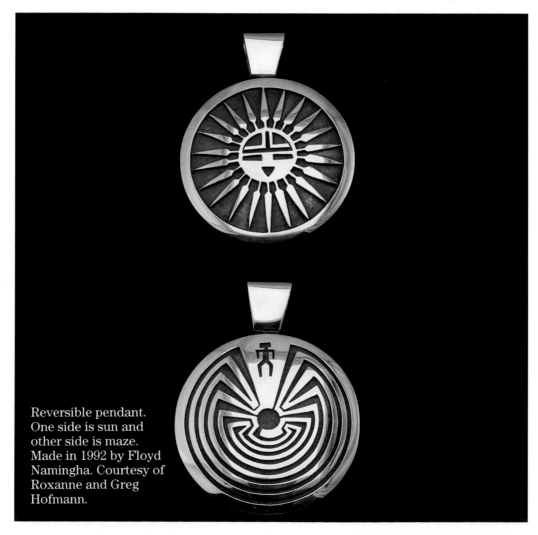

Reversible pendant. One side is sun and other side is maze. Made in 1992 by Floyd Namingha. Courtesy of Roxanne and Greg Hofmann.

Guild in 1949. The men worked at the Guild on Second Mesa or in their homes. The jewelry was sold through the Guild, thus providing a marketing outlet that would not have been possible otherwise. Fred Kabotie and his wife, Alice, managed the Guild for more than twenty years.

Charles Loloma, a student of Fred Kabotie, was the foremost innovator of contemporary Indian jewelry. In the late 1950's he was the first to use gold and precious and semiprecious stones. This completely changed the "look" of Hopi jewelry. He became internationally famous, and universally acclaimed as a genius in creating jewelry with multiple kinds of stones, using the landscape of his people for his designs. He taught his craft to his nieces, Verma Nequatewa and Sherian Honhongva, and the three became a family of artists. Today the jewelry of the two sisters is as eagerly sought after as that of their uncle Charles. Verma and Sherian exhibit their jewelry under the name of Sonwai. They not only have carried on the tradition of their uncle, but they have also developed their own styles. They too, are known internationally.

Preston Monongye was another innovator of contemporary Indian jewelry. He was born a Mission Indian, but was adopted by a Hopi family when he was seven years old. He learned the Hopi language and the techniques of silversmithing from his uncle, David Monongye, and became involved with the Kachina Society. He had a unique style of casting, and his designs differed from previous Hopi designs.

Both Charles Loloma and Preston Monongye have died, but their magnificent talents paved the way for other Indian artists.

In the 1930's silversmiths began using hallmarks on their pieces. The hallmarks identified the artists by name, by initials, or by distinctive designs. Today every piece of authentic Hopi overlay jewelry bears the hallmark of the artist. The use of gold, semiprecious and precious stones is becoming more prevalent, but the majority of Hopi jewelry is all sterling silver. Another change is the increasing number of talented women jewelry makers, however the majority of the silversmiths are still men.

The distinctivness of the Hopi overlay jewelry is well-known among the wearers of Indian jewelry and it has no peer in its uniqueness, simplicity and elegance.

Note:
All jewelry is sterling silver unless otherwise noted. All gold jewelry is 14-carat gold unless otherwise noted.

From top to bottom

Row 1

Bracelet with rectangular turquoise stone made in 1920 by Paul Saufkie.

Bracelet with four imitation turquoise stones made in 1920 by Sakhoioma.

Row 2

Bracelet with five turquoise stones made in the 1930's by Ralph Tawangyaouma.

Bracelet with one turquoise stone made in 1949 by Willie Coin.

Bracelet with one turquoise stone made in 1939-1940 by Pierce Kewanwytewa.

Row 3

Bow guard made in 1950. Silver work by Vernon Talas and leather tooling by Garland Starlie.

Child's bracelet made in 1910. Artist unknown.

Courtesy of the Museum of Northern Arizona Collection.

From Years Past

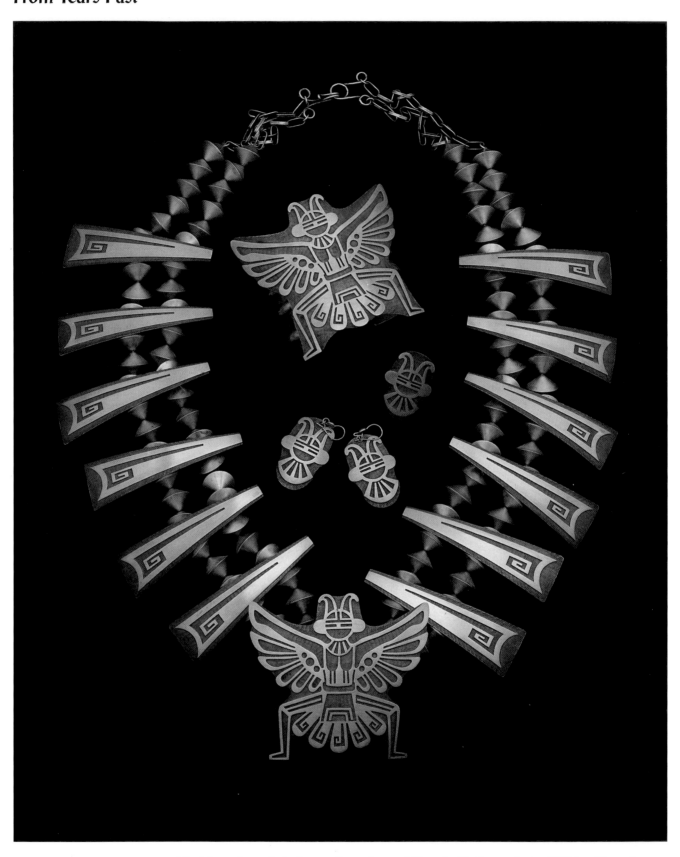

Necklace, bracelet, ring and earrings of Alosaka Deity made in 1973 by Glenn Lucas.
Courtesy of the Museum of Northern Arizona Collection.

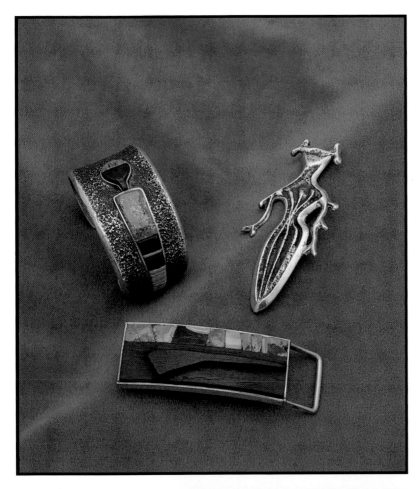

From Years Past

Cast bracelet with Morenci turquoise, coral, lapis lazuli and ironwood made in 1973.

Cast pin of Hopi Maiden made in 1968?

Belt buckle with turquoise, coral and ironwood made in 1968?

All made by Charles Loloma. Courtesy of the Museum of Northern Arizona Collection.

18-carat gold height bracelet with coral, lapis lazuli and turquoise.

18-carat gold ring with coral stone.

18-carat gold earrings with coral and turquoise.

Sterling silver earrings with coral stone.

All made in 1976 by Charles Loloma. Courtesy of Shirley and Marvin Bowman.

18-carat gold matching set consisting of a bracelet, ring, earrings and a reversible pendant made with turquoise, coral, lapis lazuli and pink coral.
See opposite page for reverse side of pendant.
All made in 1988 by Charles Loloma. Courtesy of Dine and Bob Dellenback.

Sterling silver pendant and chain with ironwood, turquoise, coral and lapis lazuli. (4½") 14-carat gold earrings with lapis lazuli.

Both made in 1975 by Charles Loloma. Courtesy of Shirley and Marvin Bowman.

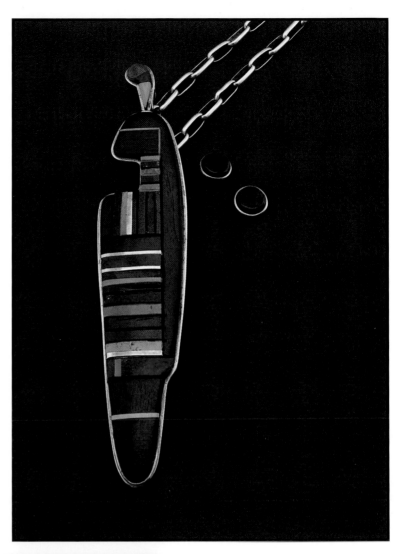

From left to right

18-carat gold ring with Landers Blue spider web turquoise made in 1975. Courtesy of Shirley and Marvin Bowman.

18-carat gold reversible pendant with Landers Blue spider web turquoise made in 1988. (See opposite page for reverse side of pendant.) Courtesy of Dine and Bob Dellenback.

14-carat gold ring with Landers Blue spider web turquoise made in 1975. Courtesy of Shirley and Marvin Bowman.

All made by Charles Loloma.

18-carat gold bracelet with turquoise and coral.
14-carat gold ring with lapis lazuli, turquoise and coral.
14-carat gold ring with turquoise stones.
All made in 1976 by Charles Loloma.
Courtesy of Shirley and Marvin Bowman.

From left to right

Sterling silver height ring with ironwood and turquoise made in 1973. Courtesy of The Galloping Goose.

14-carat gold bezel on sterling silver ring with mastodon ivory, turquoise and ironwood. Made in 1973. Private collection.

Sterling silver ring with ivory, turquoise, coral, lapis lazuli, charoite and mastodon ivory. Made in 1983. Courtesy of Selmer Collection. All made by Charles Loloma.

From the 1970's

From left to right

Row 1
Bracelet with bear paw design made by Manuel Hoyungowa.

Bracelet with peacock design and turquoise stones made by Manuel Hoyungowa.

Row 2
Bola tie of Long-haired Kachina made by Manuel Hoyungowa.

Reversible pendant with Mud Head Clown design on one side and bear paw design on the other made by Manuel Hoyungowa.

Bracelet with Corn Dancer Kachina. Artist unknown.

All courtesy of Tanner's Indian Arts.

Bracelets from the 1970's

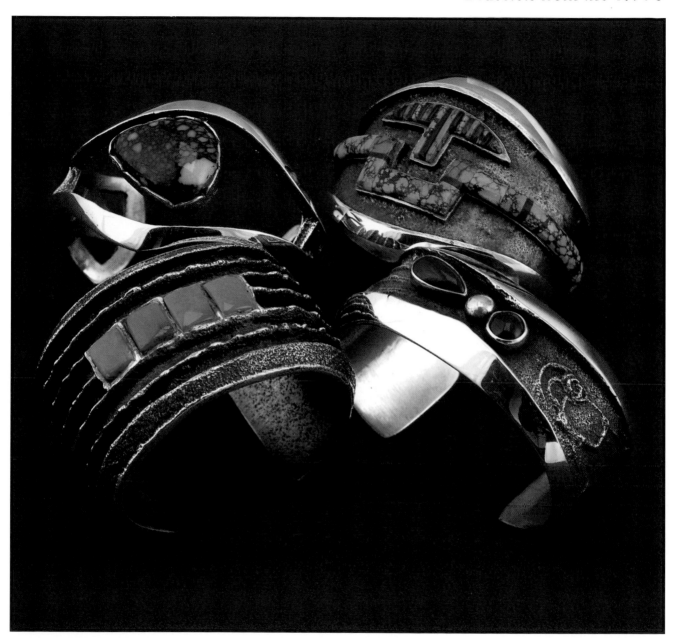

From top to bottom

Row 1

Cast with variscite stone.

Cast with four Bisbee turquoise stones.

Row 2

Cast with Chinese turquoise, coral and lapis lazuli.

Cast with two coral stones.

All made by Preston Monongye. Courtesy of Tanner's Indian Arts.

From the 1970's and 1980's

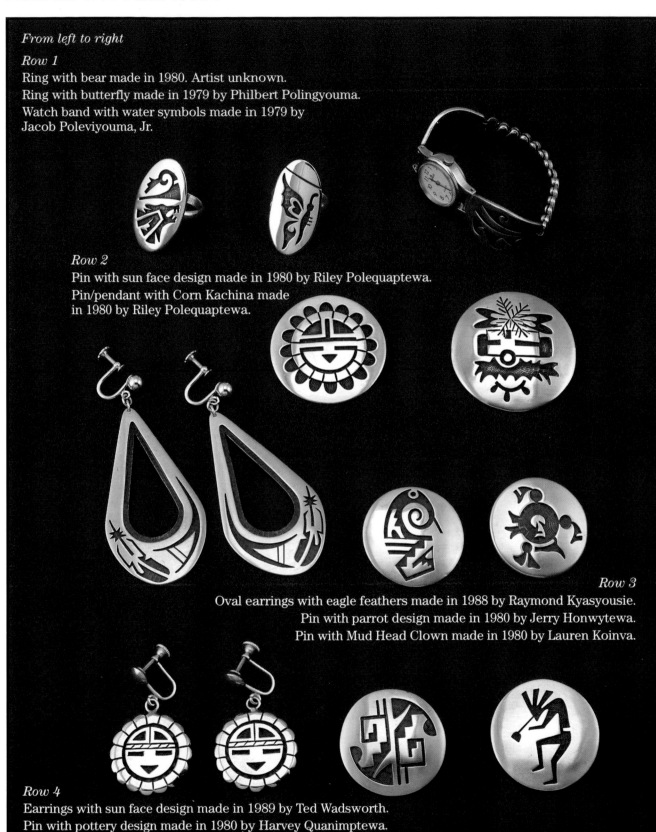

From left to right

Row 1

Ring with bear made in 1980. Artist unknown.
Ring with butterfly made in 1979 by Philbert Polingyouma.
Watch band with water symbols made in 1979 by
Jacob Poleviyouma, Jr.

Row 2

Pin with sun face design made in 1980 by Riley Polequaptewa.
Pin/pendant with Corn Kachina made
in 1980 by Riley Polequaptewa.

Row 3

Oval earrings with eagle feathers made in 1988 by Raymond Kyasyousie.
Pin with parrot design made in 1980 by Jerry Honwytewa.
Pin with Mud Head Clown made in 1980 by Lauren Koinva.

Row 4

Earrings with sun face design made in 1989 by Ted Wadsworth.
Pin with pottery design made in 1980 by Harvey Quanimptewa.
Pin with Kokopelli Kachina made in 1980 by Riley Polequaptewa.
Private collection.

Water designs, sun face and butterfly made in 1992 by Dawn Lucas.
Courtesy of Turquoise Village.

Bracelets

From top to bottom

Row 1

Bear paw made in 1992 by Robert Nequatewa. Courtesy of Turquoise Village.

Hopi village made in 1992 by Dinah and Bueford Dawahoya. Courtesy of Turquoise Village.

Salako Kachina made in 1992 by Harold Lomayaktewa. Courtesy of Turquoise Village.

Water design made in 1974. Artist unknown. Private collection.

Snakes made in 1992 by Pascal Nuvamsa. Courtesy of Turquoise Village.

Row 2

Water design made in 1992 by Robert Honyaktewa. Courtesy of Turquoise Village.

Parrot design made in 1987 by Victor Coochwytewa. Courtesy of Ula and Lee Beaudry.

Water design made in 1992 by Robert Nequatewa. Courtesy of Turquoise Village.

Water design made in 1992 by Pascal Nuvamsa. Courtesy of Turquoise Village.

Butterfly made in 1992 by Jack Nequatewa. Courtesy of Turquoise Village.

Village Scenes

Bracelet with village scene and Long-haired Kachinas made by Perry Fred.

Belt buckle with village scene and Kokopelli Kachina made by Jack Nequatewa.

Necklace with village scene made by Victor Coochwytewa.

All made in 1992. Courtesy of Turquoise Village.

Bracelets

From top to bottom

Row 1

Belt buckle and two bracelets with water designs made in 1988 by Lomawywesa (Michael Kabotie).

Row 2

Three bracelets, two with water and rain designs and one with Long-haired Kachinas made in 1992 by Phillip Honanie.

All courtesy of Museum of Northern Arizona Gift Shop.

Bracelets and Buckles

From left to right

Row 1

Belt buckle with water symbols made by Robert Lomadapki.

Lightning bracelet made by Robert Lomadapki.

Row 2

Bracelet with eagles made by Poleutyuma.

Bracelet with water symbols made by Weaver Selina.

Belt buckle of frog made by Dinah and Bueford Dawahoya.

Row 3

Bracelet of Kokopelli Kachinas with lapis lazuli stone made by Doran Sehongva.

Belt buckle of maze design made by Sidney Secakuku, Jr.

All made in 1992. Courtesy of Museum of Northern Arizona Gift Shop.

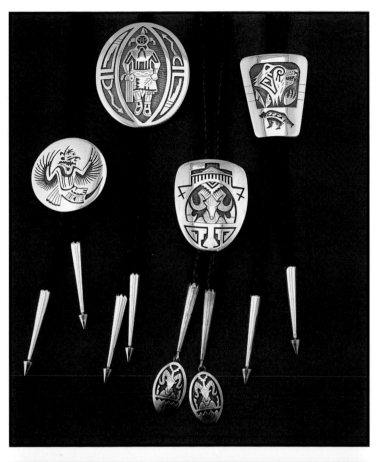

Bola Ties

From left to right

Eagle made in 1992 by Perry Fred. Courtesy of Turquoise Village.

Mud Head Clown made in 1992 by Ben Mansfield. Courtesy of Turquoise Village.

Big Horn Sheep with tips made in 1985 by Victor Coochwytewa. Courtesy of Roxanne and Greg Hofmann.

Bear made in 1992 by Verden Mansfield. Courtesy of Turquoise Village.

From left to right

Bola tie Snake Dancer made by Lawrence Saufkie. Courtesy of Turquoise Village.

Bola tie lightning, rain and clouds design with coral stone made by Lomawywesa (Michael Kabotie). Belt buckle to match above. Courtesy of Heard Museum Shop.

Bracelet with Long-haired Kachinas made by Pascal Nuvamsa. Courtesy of Turquoise Village.

All made in 1992.

Necklaces

From left to right

Row 1

Kokopelli Kachinas and corn with turquoise stone made by Pascal Nuvamsa.

Village scene made by Pascal Nuvamsa.

Row 2

Bears and sunburst made by Victor Coochwytewa.

Bears and maze made by Ben Mansfield.

Row 3

Bear, bear paws and butterflies made by Tony Burton.

All made in 1992. Courtesy of Turquoise Village.

Water designs.
Made in 1992
by Jack Seckletstewa.
Courtesy of Turquoise Village.

Necklace with corn girl pendants strung on lapis lazuli beads made by Doran Sehongva.
Left bracelet with lapis lazuli stone made by Dorothy Kyasyousie.
Right bracelet with lapis lazuli, coral and pink coral made by Roy Talaheftewa.
Middle bracelet with village scene and lapis lazuli stone made by Raymond Kyasyousie.
Earrings with rain and cloud design made by Roy Talaheftewa.
All made in 1992. Courtesy of Monongya Gallery.

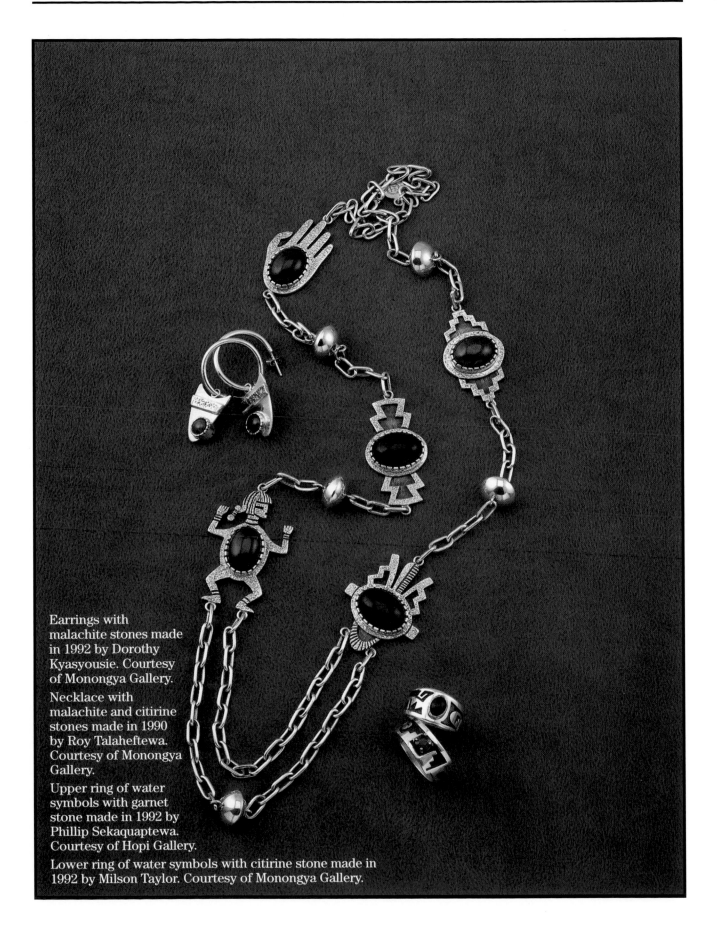

Earrings with malachite stones made in 1992 by Dorothy Kyasyousie. Courtesy of Monongya Gallery.

Necklace with malachite and citirine stones made in 1990 by Roy Talaheftewa. Courtesy of Monongya Gallery.

Upper ring of water symbols with garnet stone made in 1992 by Phillip Sekaquaptewa. Courtesy of Hopi Gallery.

Lower ring of water symbols with citirine stone made in 1992 by Milson Taylor. Courtesy of Monongya Gallery.

Necklace of parrot design made by Sharold Nutumya.

Two pair hoop earrings of parrot design made by Dawn Lucas.

Round earrings of water design made by Dawn Lucas.

Sun face earrings made by Trinidad Lucas.

All made in 1992. Courtesy of Museum of Northern Arizona Gift Shop.

From left to right

Nine-strand, white coral necklace with lapis lazuli with 14-carat gold cones and chain made by Cheryl Marie Yestewa. Courtesy of Heard Museum Shop.

Three-strand, Red Mountain turquoise necklace with 14-carat gold cones and chain made by Cheryl Marie Yestewa. Courtesy of Heard Museum Shop.

Three-strand, opal necklace with 14-carat gold cones and chain made by Cheryl Marie Yestewa. Courtesy of Heard Museum Shop.

14-carat gold ring with turquoise, lapis lazuli, pink coral, sugilite and coral made by Charles Supplee. Courtesy of Dine and Bob Dellenback.

All made in 1992.

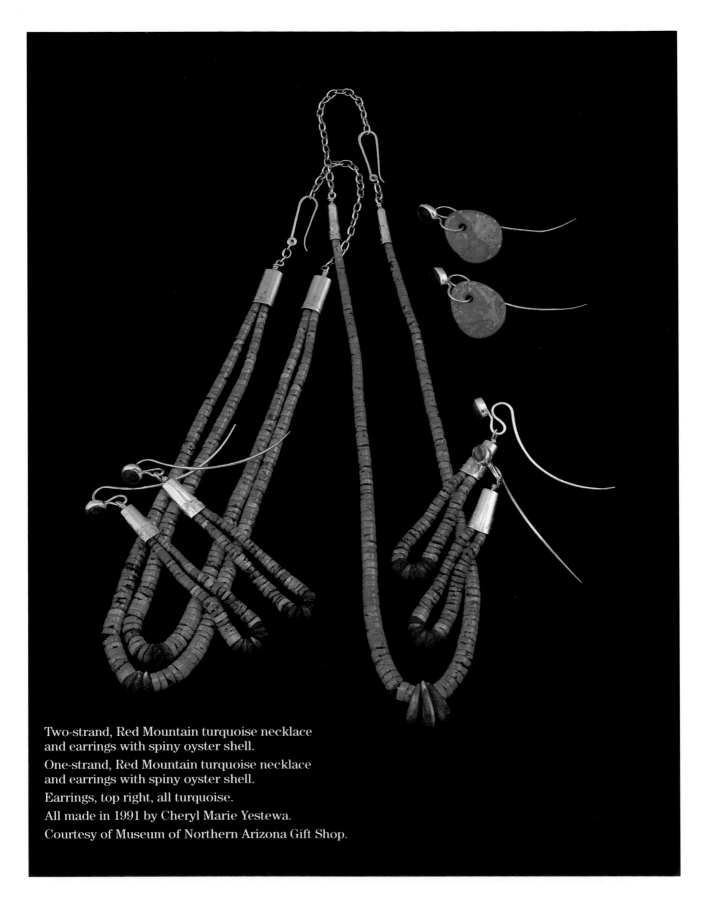

Two-strand, Red Mountain turquoise necklace
and earrings with spiny oyster shell.

One-strand, Red Mountain turquoise necklace
and earrings with spiny oyster shell.

Earrings, top right, all turquoise.

All made in 1991 by Cheryl Marie Yestewa.

Courtesy of Museum of Northern Arizona Gift Shop.

Necklace and earrings with water waves design. Necklace has coral stone. Made in 1990. Courtesy of Monongya Gallery.

Earrings of Hopi Maiden made in 1992. Courtesy of Monongya Gallery.

Earrings of bear made in 1992. Courtesy of Mae Secakuku.

Earrings of Priest made in 1992. Courtesy of Monongya Gallery.

All made by Roy Talaheftewa.

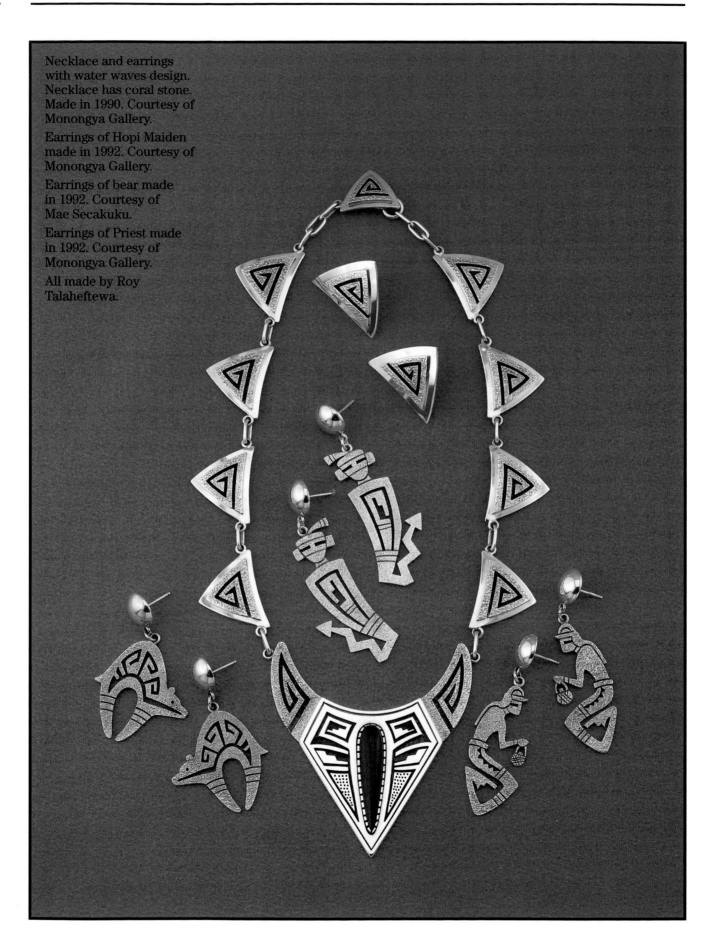

From left to right

Row 1

Earrings of Early Morning Kachina made by Art Batala.

Ring of Mud Head Clown made by Marcus Lomayestewa.

Ring of Long-haired Kachina made by Roger Selina

Row 2

Rows 2 and 3 are all rings made by Marcus Lomayestewa.

Hoho Mana Kachina.

Crow Mother Kachina.

Row 3

Kachin-mana.

Snow Maiden Kachina.

Kokopelli Mana Kachina.

Mother Kachina.

All made in 1992. Courtesy of Monongya Gallery.

Dangle Earrings

From left to right

Row 1

Corn design made by Mike Gashwazra.

Vase shaped made by Harold Lomayaktewa.

Bear paw made by Steward Dalawyma.

Row 2

Water design made by Steward Dalawyma.

Water design made by Mike Gashwazra.

Water design made by Leon Lomakema.

Row 3

Bear paw made by Mike Gashwazra.

Water design made by Leon Lomakema.

Kokopelli Kachina made by Steward Dalawyma.

Row 4

Prayer feathers design made by Steward Dalawyma.

Water design made by Steward Dalawyma.

Water design made by Marshall Lomayaktewa.

All made in 1992. Courtesy of Turquoise Village.

Post Earrings

From left to right

Row 1

Water designs made by Leon Lomakema.

Row 2

First and third pair are prayer feathers design. Second and fourth are water designs.
Made by Leon Lomakema.

Row 3

Bear paw made by Helena Namingha.

Water design made by Leon Lomakema.

Rain drop design made by Dawn Lucas.

Row 4

Kokopelli Kachina made by Helena Lomakema.

Water design made by Leon Lomakema.

Prayer feather design made by Leon Lomakema.

All made in 1992. Courtesy of Turquoise Village.

Rings

From left to right

Row 1

Corn made in 1992 by Richard Pawiki.

Roadrunner. Year and artist unknown.

Deer made in 1988 by Bueford Dawahoya.

Water design. Year and artist unknown.

Row 2

Kokopelli Kachina made in 1992. Artist unknown.

Flute player made in 1992 by Richard Pawiki.

Turquoise stone made in 1988 by Robert Lomadapki.

Bear made in 1992 by Mitchell Sockyma.

Courtesy of Museum of Northern Arizona Gift Shop.

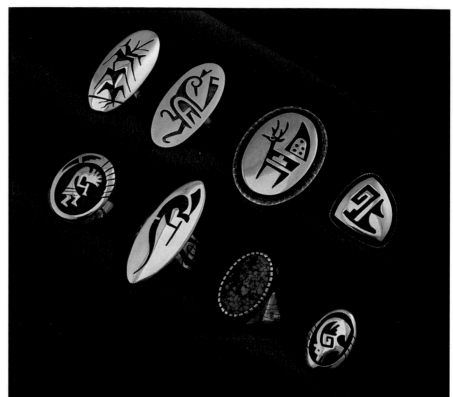

From left to right

Row 1

Water symbols made by Clifton Mowa.

Water symbols made by Julian Fred.

Prayer feathers and water symbols made by Elliot Koinva.

Water symbols made by Julian Fred.

Water symbols made by Lauren Koinva.

Row 2

Clouds made by Leroy Honyaktewa.

Prayer feathers made by Ruben Saufkie.

Bear paws made by Clifton Mowa.

Bear paw made by Darrel Pooyouma.

Water symbols. Artist unknown.

Row 3

Corn made by Edward Lomahongva.

Water symbols made by Roger Selina.

Prayer feathers made by Elliot Koinva.

Water symbols made by Jack Nequatewa.

All made in 1992. Courtesy of Monongya Gallery.

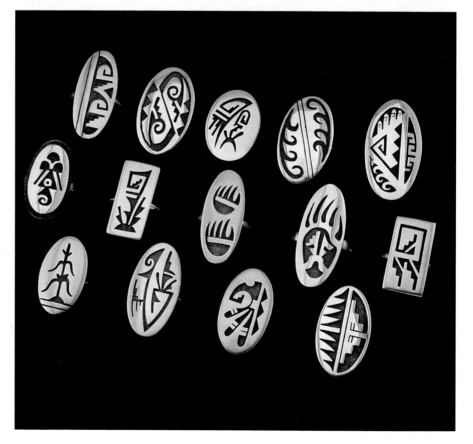

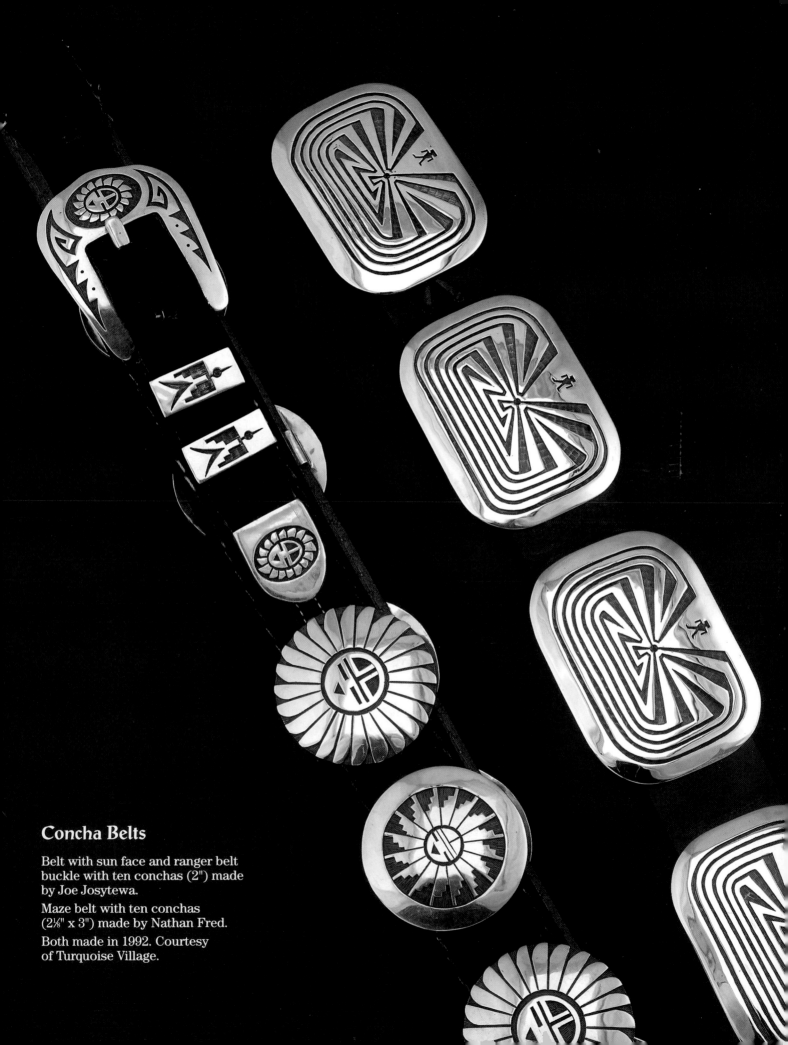

Concha Belts

Belt with sun face and ranger belt buckle with ten conchas (2") made by Joe Josytewa.

Maze belt with ten conchas (2⅛" x 3") made by Nathan Fred.

Both made in 1992. Courtesy of Turquoise Village.

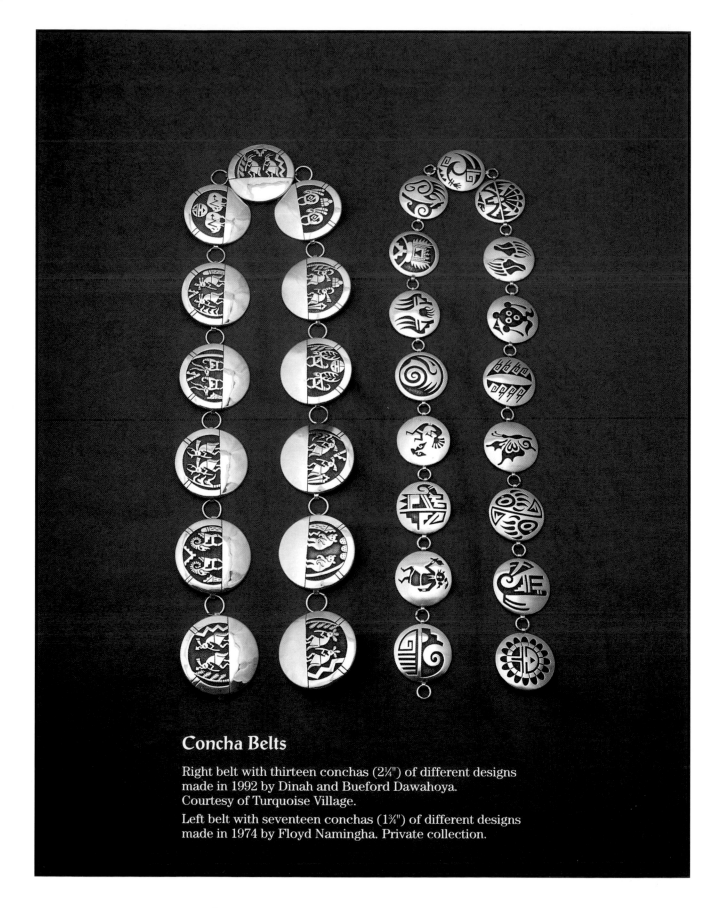

Concha Belts

Right belt with thirteen conchas (2¼") of different designs made in 1992 by Dinah and Bueford Dawahoya. Courtesy of Turquoise Village.

Left belt with seventeen conchas (1¾") of different designs made in 1974 by Floyd Namingha. Private collection.

Concha Belts

Bears with sixteen conchas (2½") and a different design on each bear made in 1992 by Joe Josytewa. Courtesy of Turquoise Village.

Parrot design with twenty three conchas (1") made in 1976. Artist unknown. Private collection.

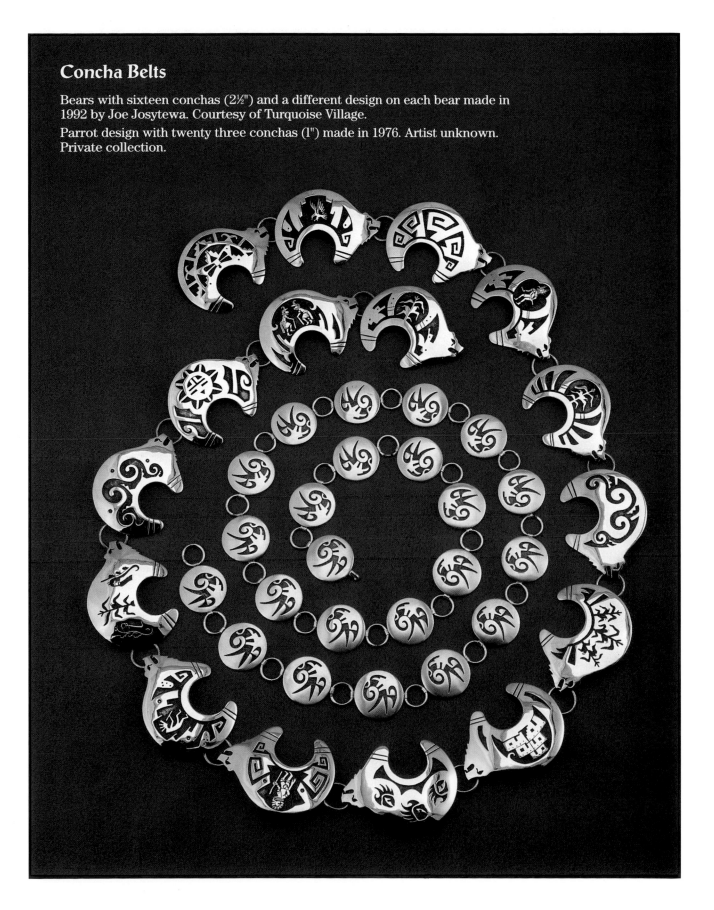

Pendants

From left to right

Pendant with corn design made in 1988 by Ramon Dalangyawma. Courtesy of Selmer Collection.

Pendant with parrot design and lapis lazuli stone made in 1992 by Cedric Kuwaninvaya. Courtesy of Monongya Gallery.

Reversible pendant with parrot design on one side and bear paw on the other made in 1977 by Milson Taylor. Private collection.

Pendant with water symbol made in 1992 by Ramon Dalangyawma. Courtesy of Monongya Gallery.

Pendant with water symbol and spiny oyster shell stone made in 1992 by Cedric Kuwaninvaya. Courtesy of Monongya Gallery.

Pendants with stones

Pendant gold on silver corn design and lapis lazuli stone made by Raymond Kyasyousie.

Pendant with sugilite stone made by Dorothy Kyasyousie.

Pendant with turquoise stone made by Dorothy Kyasyousie.

Pendant with lapis lazuli stone made by Dorothy Kyasyousie.

Pendant of water wave design with lapis lazuli stone made by Raymond Kyasyousie.

Earrings with turquoise stones made by Dorothy Kyasyousie.

Pendant of buffalo design with turquoise stone made by Dorothy Kyasyousie.

All made in 1992. Courtesy of Monongya Gallery.

Pin/Pendants

From left to right

Pin with sun, corn and village scene made in 1992 by Louie Josewytewa. Courtesy of Calnimptewa Gallery.

Pin of lizard made in 1992 by Dorothy Kyasyousie. Courtesy of Monongya Gallery.

Pendant of Crow Mother Kachina made in 1992 by Trinidad Lucas. Courtesy of Monongya Gallery.

Pendant of Kokopelli Kachina made in 1992 by Edward Lomahongva. Courtesy of Monongya Gallery.

Link bracelet with sun made in 1992 by Dawn Lucas. Courtesy of Monongya Gallery.

Earrings of Supai Uncle Kachina made in 1992 by Roy Talaheftewa. Courtesy of Monongya Gallery.

Pendant of road runner made in 1992 by Weaver Selina. Courtesy of Monongya Gallery.

Pin of Antelope made by Mark Tawahongva in 1990. Courtesy of Selmer Collection.

Necklace with water design and Chinese Mountain turquoise made in 1992 by Milson Taylor. Courtesy of Calnimptewa Gallery.

From left to right

Row 1

Pendant of Hopi Maiden made by Vern Mansfield.

Pin/pendant of bear and sun made by Dawn Lucas.

Pin of Kokopelli Mana Kachina. Artist unknown.

Row 2

Pin/pendant of flower design made by Wilmer Saufkie.

Pendant of water design made by Marshall Lomayaktewa.

Reversible pendant. One side is a ram and other side is a Kokopelli Kachina. Made by Dinah and Bueford Dawahoya.

Pin/pendant of bear paw made by Dawn Lucas.

Pin/pendant of village scene made by Quinton Laban.

Row 3

Pin/pendant of butterfly made by Dawn Lucas.

Pin of snake made by Fernando Puhuhefvaya.

Pin of corn made by Fernando Puhuhefvaya.

Pin/pendant of corn made by Dawn Lucas.

Row 4

Pendant of butterfly made by Corbin Lomakema.

Pendant of turtle made by Steward Dalawyma.

Pendant of sun made by Dawn Lucas.

Pendant of bear paw made by Corbin Lomakema.

Pendant of maze made by Ernest Honyaktewa.

All made in 1992. Courtesy of Turquoise Village.

From left to right

Row 1 Bracelet made in 1992 by Alvin Sosolda. Courtesy of Turquoise Village. Bracelet made in 1992 by Harold Lomayaktewa. Courtesy of Turquoise Village. Bracelet made in 1992 by Alvin Sosolda. Private collection.

Row 2 Belt buckle made in 1992 by Jack Seckletstewa. Courtesy of Roxanne and Greg Hofmann. Bracelet made in 1992 by Vern Mansfield. Courtesy of Turquoise Village. Bola tie made in 1982 by Glenn Lucas. Courtesy of Selmer Collection. Bola tie with tips made in 1982 by Victor Coochwytewa. Courtesy of Ula and Lee Beaudry.

Row 3 Belt buckle made in 1987 by Glenn Lucas. Courtesy of Ula and Lee Beaudry.

Row 4 Belt buckle made in 1992 by Victor Coochwytewa. Courtesy of Turquoise Village. Ranger belt buckle made in 1992 by Harold Lomayaktewa. Courtesy of Turquoise Village.

Something Different

Butterflies

Link bracelet made by Marcus Coochwykvia in 1977. Courtesy of Calnimptewa Gallery.

From top to bottom

Row 1

Ring made by Riley Polyquaptewa.

Belt buckle made by Art Batala.

Key ring made by David Mowa.

Row 2

Pendant made by Riley Polyquaptewa.

Pin/pendant. Artist unknown.

Row 3

Earrings made by Raymond Kyasyousie.

Pendant made by George Phillips.

Row 4

Earrings made by Fernanda Lomayestewa.

Key ring made by Raymond Polyquaptewa.

Money clip made by Duane Koinva.

Ring made by Clifton Mowa.

All other than link bracelet made in 1992. Courtesy of Monongya Gallery.

Spiders

Key holder, bracelet and belt buckle of spider design made by Jack Nequatewa in 1992.

Courtesy of Roxanne and Greg Hofmann.

Something Different

From top to bottom

Row 1

Cast bracelet with turquoise and coral made in 1991 by Raymond Sequaptewa. Courtesy of Museum of Northern Arizona Gift Shop.

Cast bracelet with Tibetan turquoise made in 1991 by Robert Lomadapki. Courtesy of Museum of Northern Arizona Gift Shop.

Lightning earrings made in 1984 by McBride Lomayestewa. Courtesy of Louise Riley.

Mask earrings made of oxidized sterling silver in 1992 by Raymond Sequaptewa. Courtesy of Museum of Northern Arizona Gift Shop.

Row 2

Bracelet with turquoise stone made in 1981 by Duane Maktima. Courtesy of Louise Riley.

Cherrywood earrings with malachite stones made in 1984 by Marvin Lomahaftewa. Courtesy of Louise Riley.

Cottonwood earrings with turquoise stones made in 1984 by Marcus Lomayestewa. Courtesy of Louise Riley.

Earrings of turquoise and spiny oyster shell made in 1990 by Cheryl Marie Yestewa. Courtesy of Museum of Northern Arizona Gift Shop.

Mask earrings made of oxidized sterling silver in 1992 made by Raymond Sequaptewa. Courtesy of Museum of Northern Arizona Gift Shop.

Something Different

From left to right

Necklace with pink coral, azurite and variscite strung on coral, lapis lazuli, chrysocolla and azurite beads made in 1990 by Phillip Sekaquaptewa. Private collection.

Cross with Bisbee turquoise made in 1970 by Preston Monongye. Courtesy of Roxanne and Greg Hofmann.

Bola tie cast and drop silver with jasper, coral and turquoise stones made in 1990. Courtesy of Ula and Lee Beaudry.

Mask ring of lapis lazuli, antler, sugilite and ivory made in 1990. Courtesy of Ula and Lee Beaudry.

Pendant with lapis lazuli stone and strung on lapis lazuli beads with alternating silver. Matching ring. Made in 1991 by Phillip Sekaquaptewa. Courtesy of Selmer Collection.

Something Different

From left to right

Row 1
Miniature seed bowl made in 1992.
Indian with feathered headdress pin made in 1992.
Miniature seed bowl made in 1991.

Row 2
Ranger belt buckle made in 1992.

Row 3
Hummingbird pin made in 1992.
Earrings made in 1992.
All made by Howard Sice.
Courtesy of Museum of Northern Arizona Gift Shop.

From top to bottom

Row 1

Eagle pin made by Mark Tawahongva.

Split-twig earrings made by Ramson Lomatewama.*

Buffalo pin/pendant made by Norman Honie, Sr.

Row 2

Early Morning Kachina pin. Artist unknown.

Split-twig pin and key chain made by
Ramson Lomatewama.*

Flute player pin with charoite stone made
by Milson Taylor.

Row 3

Ladybug pin made by Norman Honie.

Split-twig pendant made by Ramson Lomatewama.*

Pendant with turquoise stone made by
Robert Lomadapki.

All made in 1992 with exception of flute player pin
made in 1991. Courtesy of Museum of Northern
Arizona Gift Shop.

*Split-twig figurines were originally made of wood and
were first discovered in 1933 in a side canyon in the
Grand Canyon. They are estimated to be 2500 to 8000
years old.

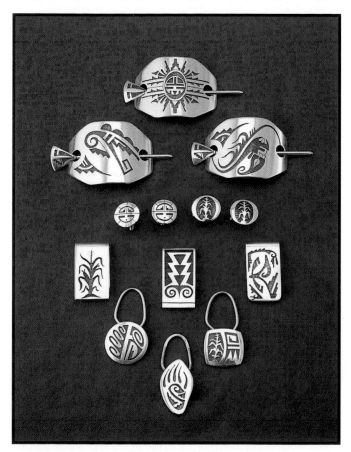

From left to right

Row 1

Hair pieces of sun face, water design and Long-
haired Kachina made by Leon Lomakema.

Row 2

Cuff links sun face design made by Dawn Lucas.

Cuff links corn design made by Roy Wing.

Row 3

Money clip corn design made by Dawn Lucas.

Money clip water design made by Merle Sehongva.

Money clip prayer feather design made by
Tony Burton.

Row 4

Key ring water design made by by Andrew Saufkie.

Key ring bear paw made by Julian Fred.

Key ring corn design made by Perry Fred.

All made in 1992. Courtesy of Turquoise Village.

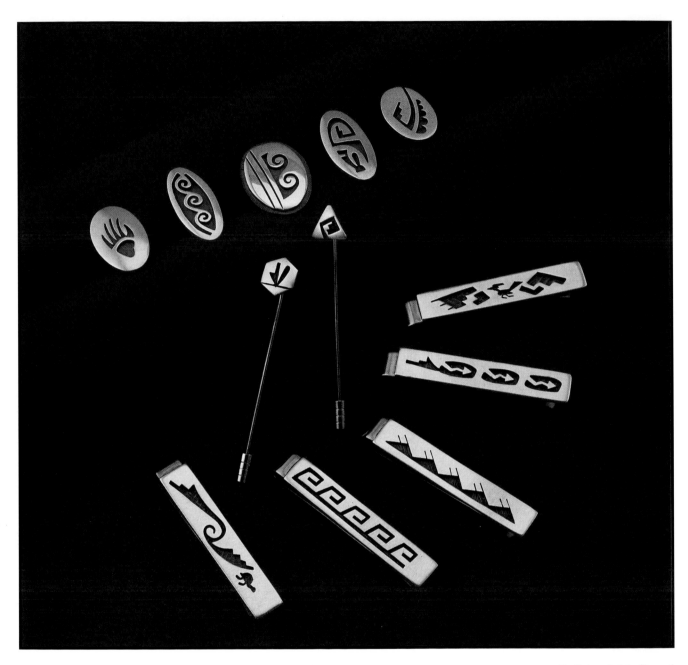

Left to right, Row 1

Row 1—Tie Tacks
Bear paw by Vinton Selina.
Water design by Vinton Selina.
Water design by Mark Tawahongva.
Water design and prayer feather design by Vinton Selina.
Water design by Vinton Selina.

Row 2—Stick Pins
Upper, prayer feather symbol.
Lower, water design.

Row 3—Tie Bars
All are water designs.
Stick pins and tie bars are by Raymond Kyasyousie.
All made in 1992. Courtesy of Monongya Gallery.

From left to right

Row 1—Rings

Water symbol made by Terry Wadsworth. Water symbol made by Leroy Honyaktewa. Prayer feather design made by Elliot Koinva. Water symbol made by Elliot Koinva. Water symbol made by Elliot Koinva.

Row 2—Rings

Water symbol made by Terry Wadsworth. Water symbol made by Sharold Nutumya. Water symbol made by Terry Wadsworth. Water symbol made by Terry Wadsworth. Prayer feather design. Artist unknown.

Row 3—Key rings

Spider made by Roger Selina. Snake Dancer made by Edward Lomahongva. Eagle made by Terry Wadsworth.

All made in 1992. Courtesy of Monongya Gallery.

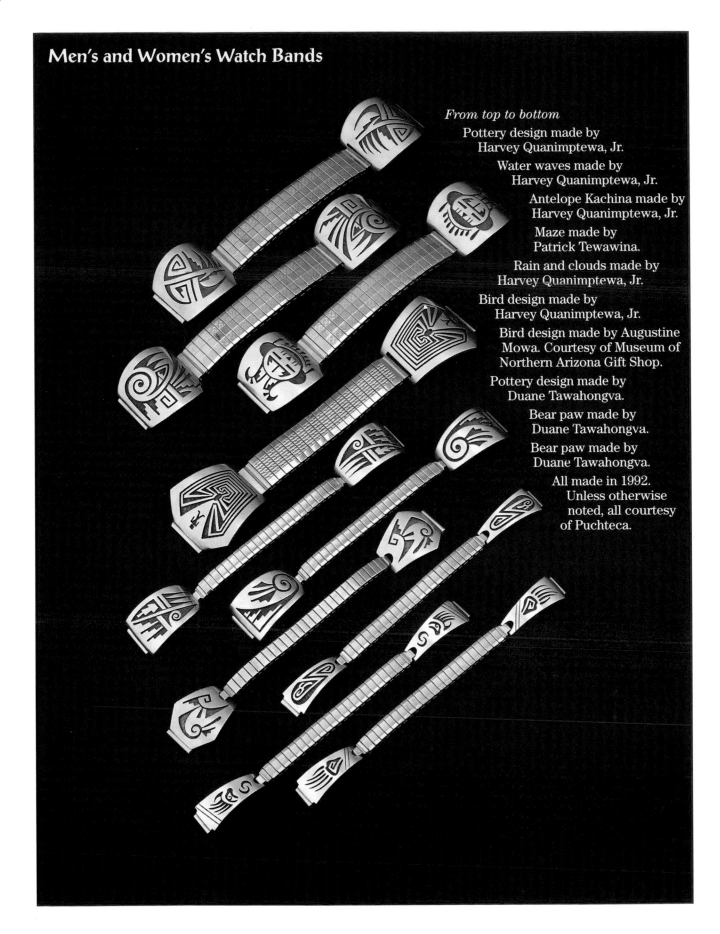

Men's and Women's Watch Bands

From top to bottom

Pottery design made by
Harvey Quanimptewa, Jr.

Water waves made by
Harvey Quanimptewa, Jr.

Antelope Kachina made by
Harvey Quanimptewa, Jr.

Maze made by
Patrick Tewawina.

Rain and clouds made by
Harvey Quanimptewa, Jr.

Bird design made by
Harvey Quanimptewa, Jr.

Bird design made by Augustine
Mowa. Courtesy of Museum of
Northern Arizona Gift Shop.

Pottery design made by
Duane Tawahongva.

Bear paw made by
Duane Tawahongva.

Bear paw made by
Duane Tawahongva.

All made in 1992.
Unless otherwise
noted, all courtesy
of Puchteca.

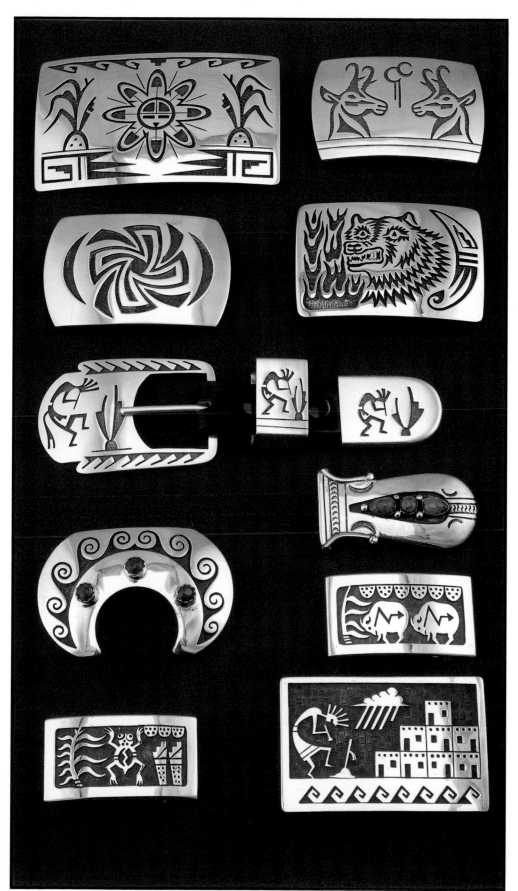

Belt Buckles

From top to bottom

Row 1

Sun face and corn made in 1992 by Jack Nequatewa. Courtesy of Turquoise Village.

Whirlwind made in 1992 by George Phillips. Courtesy of Turquoise Village.

Ranger belt buckle with Kokopelli Kachinas made in 1992 by Harold Lomayaktewa. Courtesy of Turquoise Village.

Rain drop design with three coral stones made in 1992 by Harold Lomayaktewa. Courtesy of Roxanne and Greg Hofmann.

Frog and corn made in 1992 by Dinah and Bueford Dawahoya. Courtesy of Turquoise Village.

Row 2

Deer made in 1992 by Ben Mansfield. Private collection.

Bear made in 1992 by Louis Quiyo. Courtesy of Turquoise Village.

Oval with three turquoise stones made in 1951 by Morris Robinson. Courtesy of Roxanne and Greg Hofmann.

Buffalo made in 1992 by Dinah and Bueford Dawahoya. Courtesy of Turquoise Village.

Kokopelli Kachina and village made in 1992 by Jack Nequatewa. Private collection.

Bracelet with pottery design made by Julian Fred.

Spider pin made by Emery Holmes.

Necklace with water symbols and turquoise stone made by Eldon Kalemsa, Sr.

Two bear paw and one Kokopelli Kachina rings, gold on silver made by Milson Taylor.

Pendant with Kokopelli Kachina, gold on silver made by Marvin Lucas.

All made in 1992. Courtesy of Monongya Gallery.

From left to right

Three-strand necklace of lapis lazuli,pink coral and fresh water pearl made in 1992. Courtesy of Beverly Sekaquaptewa.

Bracelet gold on silver with petroglyph figures and Kokopelli Kachina with lapis lazuli and cocoa bolo wood made in 1993. Courtesy of Hopi Gallery.

Necklace with Crow Mother Kachina of shattuckite, pink coral and fresh water pearl made in 1992. Courtesy of Southwest Gallery.

Bracelet of Kokopelli Kachina and Antelope Kachina of malachite, pink coral and cocoa bolo wood made in 1992. Courtesy of Gordon Graff.

All made by Phillip Sekaquaptewa.

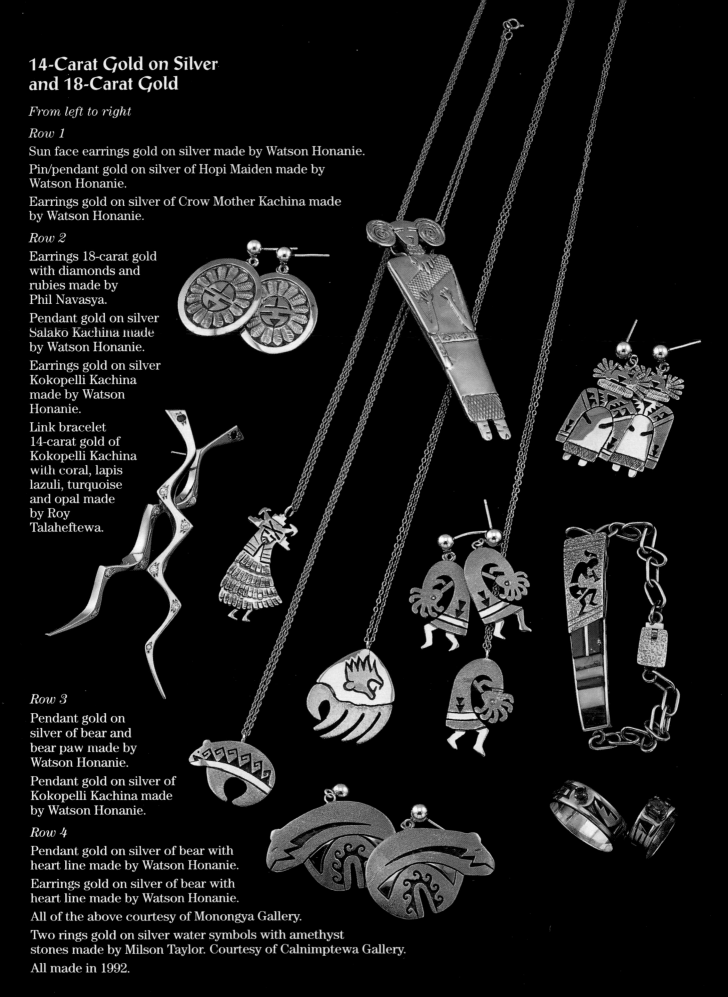

14-Carat Gold on Silver and 18-Carat Gold

From left to right

Row 1

Sun face earrings gold on silver made by Watson Honanie.

Pin/pendant gold on silver of Hopi Maiden made by Watson Honanie.

Earrings gold on silver of Crow Mother Kachina made by Watson Honanie.

Row 2

Earrings 18-carat gold with diamonds and rubies made by Phil Navasya.

Pendant gold on silver Salako Kachina made by Watson Honanie.

Earrings gold on silver Kokopelli Kachina made by Watson Honanie.

Link bracelet 14-carat gold of Kokopelli Kachina with coral, lapis lazuli, turquoise and opal made by Roy Talaheftewa.

Row 3

Pendant gold on silver of bear and bear paw made by Watson Honanie.

Pendant gold on silver of Kokopelli Kachina made by Watson Honanie.

Row 4

Pendant gold on silver of bear with heart line made by Watson Honanie.

Earrings gold on silver of bear with heart line made by Watson Honanie.

All of the above courtesy of Monongya Gallery.

Two rings gold on silver water symbols with amethyst stones made by Milson Taylor. Courtesy of Calnimptewa Gallery.

All made in 1992.

48

14-Carat Gold on Silver

Bracelet studded with diamonds made in 1991
Lower bracelet of village scene made in 1992
Ring of Salako Kachina made in 1991
Chain and pendant of eagle made in 1992
Earrings of village scene made in 1991.
Earrings made by Ricky Coochwytewa. All else made by Victor Coochwytewa.
Courtesy of Museum of Northern Arizona Gift Shop.

Reversible Pendants

14-Carat Gold on Silver

Round pendant with silver sun face on one side and village scene with gold moon on the other side.

Rectangular pendant with village scene and gold moon on one side and bear paw on the other side.

Gold is on the pad of the bear paw.

Both made in 1991 by John Coochyumptewa. Courtesy of Turquoise Village.

14-Carat Gold on Silver

Top bracelet with Long-haired Kachinas made in 1992 by Pascal Nuvamsa. Courtesy of Turquoise Village.

Lower bracelet with bears made in 1992 by Andrew Saufkie. Courtesy of Turquoise Village.

Belt buckle maze design with Kokopelli Kachinas made in 1992 by Joe Josytewa. Courtesy of Al Myman.

Oval ring maze design made in 1991 by Jason Takala. Courtesy of Al Myman.

Square ring maze design made in 1992 by Joe Josytewa. Courtesy of Turquoise Village.

Two pins made in 1992 by Moody Lomayaktewa. Courtesy of Turquoise Village.

Long earrings corn design made in 1992 by Joe Josytewa. Courtesy of Turquoise Village.

Square earrings water design made in 1992 by Moody Lomayaktewa. Courtesy of Turquoise Village.

All 14-Carat Gold on Silver

From top to bottom

Row 1

Bracelet with deer. Bracelet with eagle. Bracelet with eagles.

Row 2

Bracelet with buffalo, big horn sheep and bear. Bracelet with village scene.Bracelet with village scene.
Chain and pendant of Kachin-mana. All made in 1992 by Watson Honanie. Courtesy of Monongya Gallery.

Matching set of bola tie and belt buckle. 18-carat gold with turquoise, coral and lapis lazuli. Made in 1992 by Sonwai. Courtesy of Dine and Bob Dellenback.

18-carat gold pendant (3¾") with pink coral, turquoise, lapis lazuli, coral and sugilite.

18-carat gold earrings with turquoise, coral, lapis lazuli and sugilite.

Both made in 1990 by Sonwai. Courtesy of Shirley and Marvin Bowman.

Matching Set

14-carat gold pendant (4") with pink coral, turquoise, lapis lazuli, coral and sugilite.

From left to right

18-carat gold height bracelet with charoite, lapis lazuli, turquoise and coral.

14-carat gold ring with charoite, lapis lazuli, coral, turquoise and sugilite.

14-carat gold ring (2") with charoite, lapis lazuli, coral, turquoise and sugilite.

All made in 1990 by Sonwai. Courtesy of Shirley and Marvin Bowman.

The Author

Backpacking and river-running exploits led Theda Bassman into Arizona where she met the Hopi Indians. Their feelings for nature and environment were so similar to hers that she developed many friendships with them in a short period of time. For the past forty-five years she has traveled to the Hopi mesas, not only to visit her Hopi friends, but also to buy their crafts. In 1972 she opened a gallery in Beverly Hills called "The Indian and I." When she and her husband retired, they moved to Palm Desert, California where they now live. They also have a cabin on the Mogollon Rim in Northern Arizona, where they spend their time in the forest and traveling to the nearby Hopi mesas. Theda Bassman is a feminist, an environmentalist and a lover of chamber music. She is a member of Greenpeace, The Sierra Club, Hemlock and Hospice. This is her third book.

The Photographer

Gene Balzer is a Professor of Photography at the University of Northern Arizona in Flagstaff, Arizona. He photographs the majority of the collection of the Museum of Northern Arizona based in Flagstaff, Arizona and conducts field trips for them to various archeological sites and National Parks on the Colorado Plateau. His photographs have appeared in the *Arizona Highways*, American Indian Art Magazine, Southwest Profile, Plateau Magazine, The World and I and The Indian Country Guide. His photograph was used for the cover of the CD of Native American Flute Player, R. Carlos Nakai. He also was the photographer for Theda Bassman's book, *Hopi Kachina Dolls and their Carvers* and for Theda and Michael Bassman's book, *Zuni Jewelry*.

Index of Artists

Back Cover Photo

Bracelet with snake and pot made by Eldon James in 1973. Courtesy of Gary Newman.

Belt buckle with deer and corn made by Jack Nequatewa in 1992. Courtesy of Turquoise Village.

Pin with bear made by Caroline Fred in 1992. Courtesy of Turquoise Village.

Belt buckle with sun and eagle made by Raymond Namingha in 1992. Courtesy of Turquoise Village.

Bracelet with butterfly made by Jack Nequatewa in 1992. Courtesy of Turquoise Village.